PROTECT AND STRENGTHEN YOUR BORDERS

Natural and Spiritual Defense for Kingdom-Minded Believers

PASTOR DR. CLAUDINE BENJAMIN

For more information or to book an event, contact:
inspiredtowinsouls@gmail.com

Published by:

Editor: Cleveland O. McLeish (Author C. Orville McLeish)

ISBN: 978-1-965635-35-3 (paperback)

Dedication

To the gatekeepers, the watchmen, the intercessors, and the wall-builders—This book is for you.

To every believer who has stood in the gap when others walked away.

To every parent who has prayed through the night to protect their household.

To every leader who refused to lower the standard even when the cost was great; May your hands be strengthened, your vision sharpened, and your voice restored.

Above all, to the One who is our Strong Tower, our Fortress, and our Defender—Jesus Christ, the Chief Cornerstone—This book is dedicated to You. May every word bring glory to Your Name and awaken the body to rise and build again.

Acknowledgments

To my heavenly Father, You are my Fortress, my Defender, and my ever-present Help. Thank You for entrusting me with this message and for the anointing that empowers me to write, teach, and minister. This book is for Your glory.

To the Holy Spirit, Thank You for the revelation, wisdom, and discernment that guided every page. You are the true Author behind this work.

To my family, Thank you for your unwavering love, support, and patience. Your prayers, encouragement, and understanding have made this journey possible. You are my first ministry and forever my greatest blessing.

To my spiritual covering, mentors, and prayer warriors, thank you for standing on the wall with me. Your spiritual insight, guidance, and intercession helped birth and protect this assignment. I am honored to walk alongside you in the kingdom.

To every reader, builder, and believer, You are the reason this book was written. May it ignite your faith, stir your spirit, and empower you to stand boldly in the place God has assigned you. Your obedience matters—your border matters.

Finally, to every person who has ever felt the weight of spiritual warfare or the urgency to protect what God has given you, this is your reminder: **You are not alone. You are not defenseless. You are divinely equipped.** Now rise and guard your border.

With gratitude,
Pastor Claudine Benjamin

About the Author

Pastor Claudine Benjamin is a passionate preacher, teacher, and author dedicated to equipping the Body of Christ with biblical truth and spiritual strategies for victorious living. With a prophetic voice and a pastoral heart, she boldly declares the Word of God to awaken, warn, and empower believers to guard their spiritual territory and walk in divine authority.

In her latest book, Protect and Strengthen Your Border, Pastor Claudine delivers a timely message to the church: now more than ever, we must recognize the enemy's tactics, defend what God has entrusted to us, and establish strong spiritual boundaries through prayer, discernment, and obedience.

With years of ministry experience and a burden for spiritual restoration, she ministers with transparency and conviction, often drawing from real-life experiences, biblical examples, and divine revelation. Her writing is both prophetic and practical—designed to stir readers into action and deeper intimacy with Christ.

Pastor Claudine continues to serve faithfully in her local church and beyond, mentoring leaders, interceding for revival, and calling God's people to rise up, build up, and stay spiritually fortified.

Table of Contents

Chapter 1

The Mandate to Build Strong Borders

Understanding God's Call To Guard What Is Sacred

"So we built the wall, and the entire wall was joined together up to half its height, for the people had a mind to work." — Nehemiah 4:6 (NKJV)

God is a God of order, structure, and boundaries. From the beginning of creation, He established borders—He separated light from darkness, land from sea, and holiness from impurity. These divine borders serve to protect, to preserve, and to define what belongs to Him. In the same way, you and I are called to build and fortify spiritual and natural borders in our lives.

In Nehemiah's time, the walls of Jerusalem had been broken down, leaving the people vulnerable to ridicule and attack. But Nehemiah received a burden from God, not just to rebuild a wall of stone, but to restore dignity, safety, and divine order. Today, God is placing that same burden in the hearts of His people. It is time to inspect the gates, assess the damage, and commit to rebuilding.

The mandate to build strong borders is not optional—it is urgent. Without spiritual borders, the enemy finds easy access. Without natural boundaries in relationships, finances, ministry, and morality, chaos can quickly reign. God has called you to be a builder, a protector, and a restorer.

Be challenged to assess the condition of your personal, family, and ministry borders. Are the walls intact? Are there broken places? Has the gate been left open? Like Nehemiah, you must respond to the call with action and faith.

Scriptures for Reflection

- Nehemiah 1:3-4
- Nehemiah 2:17-20
- Proverbs 25:28
- Isaiah 58:12

Chapter 2

Natural Borders – The Principle of Protection

How Physical Boundaries Teach Spiritual Truth

"When the Most High gave to the nations their inheritance, when He divided mankind, He fixed the borders of the peoples according to the number of the sons of God." — Deuteronomy 32:8 (ESV)

God is the Original Architect of Borders

From the Garden of Eden, God established natural perimeters for humanity's dwelling, dominion, and destiny. Adam was placed *within* Eden, not to wander aimlessly, but to tend and keep a specifically designated territory (**see Genesis 2:15**). Borders are not man's invention—they are God's design to create structure, establish identity, and provide protection.

Just as God separated waters from land and nations by boundaries (**see Acts 17:26**), He uses natural borders to reflect His spiritual patterns. When we respect borders, we respect the wisdom and sovereignty of God.

The Purpose of Natural Boundaries

Natural borders do several critical things:

- **They Define Ownership**: Property lines determine who owns what. Spiritually, your "territory" includes your mind, heart, home, and calling.

- **They Prevent Unwanted Intrusion**: Walls, fences, and national borders protect against danger. The absence of boundaries invites chaos and attack.

- **They Encourage Stewardship**: When people know what belongs to them, they care for it more responsibly.

Scripture shows us that borders were a blessing from God. The tribes of Israel were given land with boundaries (**see Numbers 34**), and even God placed cherubim and a flaming sword to guard Eden after the fall (**see Genesis 3:24**).

When Borders are Ignored or Violated

One of the first sins against borders was Cain's refusal to accept boundaries. He not only crossed moral lines but rejected God's correction. His punishment? He became a restless wanderer—without direction, boundary, or peace (**see Genesis 4:12**).

When King Ahab coveted Naboth's vineyard, he crossed a natural and ancestral boundary with evil intent—and paid the price (**see 1 Kings 21**).

Ignoring natural borders leads to spiritual and emotional disorder. God expects us to *honor* the lines He has drawn.

God Uses Borders to Separate and Sanctify

Natural borders also serve as tools of consecration. God separated Israel from pagan nations with literal and moral boundaries. Holiness requires separation—not isolation, but distinction. Natural borders create space for identity and sanctification.

As believers, we must understand that our physical space, our time, our body, and even our conversations must have boundaries. We are set apart, and that sanctification should be reflected in every area of our lives.

Respecting Others' Borders

Just as you protect your own borders, you must also learn to honor the borders God has set around others. This includes:

- Respecting physical property.
- Honoring emotional and relational boundaries.
- Not overstepping roles and responsibilities in ministry or leadership.

The anointing flows best within the order of God. Chaos and offense arise when lines are crossed without God's permission.

Natural Borders Are Divine Patterns

God gives us visible signs to teach invisible truths. Natural borders are more than property lines—they are divine illustrations of God's wisdom, protection, and desire for order. Before you can strengthen your spiritual borders, you must first understand and respect the principle of natural ones.

Scriptures for Meditation

- Deuteronomy 32:8
- Genesis 2:15
- Acts 17:26
- Numbers 34:1-13
- Proverbs 22:28
- Psalm 16:6

Chapter 3

Spiritual Borders – Guarding Your Mind, Heart, and Soul

Establishing Holy Boundaries Against Spiritual Invasion

"Above all else, guard your heart, for everything you do flows from it." — Proverbs 4:23 (NIV)

The Invisible War for the Soul

We are not merely physical beings—we are spirit, soul, and body. While natural borders are seen, spiritual borders must be discerned and diligently maintained. There is a constant battle for your mind, emotions, and spirit. Satan's strategy is subtle: he infiltrates, influences, and invades the unguarded areas of your life.

The Apostle Paul warns, **"Do not give place to the devil" (Ephesians 4:27).** The enemy needs an open gate, a broken wall, or a cracked foundation to gain access. This is why building and maintaining strong spiritual borders is vital for victorious living.

Guarding the Mind: The Battlefield of Thoughts

The mind is the entry point of most spiritual attacks. Negative thinking, doubt, fear, temptation, and deception all begin in the thought realm.

- **Set Your Mind**: "**Set your minds on things above, not on earthly things.**" **(Colossians 3:2 - NIV).**

- **Renew Your Mind**: **Romans 12:2** urges us to be transformed by renewing our minds with God's truth.

- **Take Every Thought Captive**: "...bringing every thought into captivity to the obedience of Christ" (**see 2 Corinthians 10:5**).

A guarded mind is a mind aligned with truth, peace, and purpose.

Guarding the Heart: The Wellspring of Life

The heart is the seat of emotions, motives, and desires. If the heart is unguarded, bitterness, offense, lust, pride, and hatred can fester.

- **Check for Contamination**: "**Create in me a clean heart, O God...**" **(Psalm 51:10 - NKJV).**

- **Protect Your Passion**: Don't let worldly influences steal your zeal for God.

- **Anchor Your Affections**: "**Where your treasure is, there your heart will be also.**" **(Matthew 6:21 - NKJV).**

To guard your heart means to monitor what you love, what you chase, and what you tolerate.

Guarding the Soul: Your Eternal Identity

Your soul—your will, emotions, and intellect—needs covering. It is your spiritual identity in Christ that the enemy seeks to distort. When your soul is exposed, you risk losing your spiritual direction and divine focus.

- **Rest for the Soul**: **"You will find rest for your souls."** **(Matthew 11:29 - NKJV).**

- **Protection through Submission**: **"Therefore submit to God. Resist the devil and he will flee from you." (James 4:7 - NKJV).**

- **Reinforce with the Word**: The Word of God strengthens the soul against compromise and deception.

Spiritual Borders are Built with Intentionality

Just like Nehemiah had to *rise and build* the wall, you must choose to set up personal spiritual boundaries:

- Limit toxic conversations and ungodly media.
- Set times of prayer and fasting.
- Establish accountability and spiritual mentorship.
- Say "no" to temptations and distractions.

A casual believer is a vulnerable one. Strong borders require strong decisions.

When Borders Break: The Signs of Invasion

How do you know your spiritual borders have been compromised?

- You're easily offended.
- You're spiritually dry or disconnected.
- Sin is no longer convicting.
- Fear and confusion dominate your thoughts.
- You avoid prayer and the Word.

These are warning signs. But with repentance, spiritual discipline, and restoration, your borders can be rebuilt stronger than before.

Guard What God Has Entrusted to You

Your life is valuable. Your calling is sacred. Your relationship with God is worth protecting. Let no enemy cross the lines God has set for your protection. Build, guard, and maintain your spiritual borders—because everything else flows from them.

Scriptures for Meditation

- Proverbs 4:23
- 2 Corinthians 10:4–5
- Ephesians 6:11–13
- Psalm 119:11
- James 4:7
- Romans 13:14
- Philippians 4:7–8

Chapter 4

Broken Borders – What Happens When the Hedge is Breached

Recognizing Vulnerability And Reclaiming Dominion

"And whoever breaks through a wall will be bitten by a serpent." — Ecclesiastes 10:8b (NKJV)

The Danger of Neglecting Your Border

Spiritual borders are not permanent unless maintained. Just as physical fences wear down over time and exposure, spiritual borders can erode if neglected. Laziness in prayer, compromise in values, and tolerance of sin weaken the hedge God placed around you.

Hosea 4:6 declares, **"My people are destroyed for lack of knowledge." (NKJV).** Destruction doesn't always come through violent attack—it often begins through subtle erosion. We must regularly examine the walls surrounding our spiritual life, family, purpose, and purity.

The Breach Creates an Entry Point for the Enemy

The enemy is always looking for an opening. When the wall is broken, invasion is inevitable.

- **Legal Access Through Sin**: Sin opens the gate for the enemy to legally operate in our lives. "Give no place to the devil." **(see Ephesians 4:27)**.

- **Unhealed Wounds and Offense**: Offense creates cracks in our emotional and spiritual walls. Bitterness becomes a breeding ground for spiritual warfare.

- **Compromise Weakens Conviction**: Every time you make peace with sin, your wall gets lower.

Just as a city without walls is defenseless, a believer without spiritual boundaries becomes prey.

The Consequences of a Breached Border

When your spiritual hedge is broken, several things begin to manifest:

- **Confusion and Chaos: "God is not the author of confusion" (1 Corinthians 14:33 - NKJV).**

- **Uninvited Warfare**: The enemy launches attacks in areas you were once strong in.

- **Spiritual Leakage**: You lose your joy, peace, vision, and strength.

- **Loss of Authority**: Samson didn't lose his strength when his hair was cut—he lost it when his consecration was breached **(see Judges 16)**.

How to Identify a Breach in Your Wall

God will often alert you when a wall is compromised. Ask yourself:

- Am I more vulnerable to temptation than I used to be?
- Is my prayer life decreasing?
- Have I stopped hearing from God clearly?
- Are my relationships showing signs of attack?
- Do I feel spiritually uncovered or unsafe?

The first step to restoration is *recognition*. You can't fix what you won't face.

Rebuilding the Broken Places

The good news? Broken borders can be restored with God's help. Like Nehemiah, we must *rise up and build* with urgency and intentionality.

- **Repent and Renounce**: Repent for allowing the breach and renounce every illegal access point (**see Joel 2:12-13**).

- **Pray and Fast**: These spiritual tools are weapons for wall-repair.

- **Reinforce with the Word**: Return to the Word of God as your foundation (**see Psalm 119:105**).

- **Set Watchmen**: Establish accountability and spiritual covering in your life.

Isaiah 58:12 says, **"Those from among you shall build the old waste places; You shall raise up the foundations of many generations..." (NKJV).**

Restoring Dominion and Boundary Authority

Once your walls are rebuilt, it's time to enforce your spiritual authority. Do not allow the enemy to steal your identity, calling, or peace again. Stand firm in your role as a gatekeeper, priest, and intercessor over your life, family, ministry, and territory.

Declare as Job did: **"You have hedged me in behind and before, and laid Your hand upon me." — Psalm 139:5 (NKJV).**

Scriptures for Meditation

- Ecclesiastes 10:8
- Ezekiel 22:30
- Job 1:10
- Nehemiah 4:7–9
- Joel 2:12–13
- Isaiah 58:12
- Judges 16
- Ephesians 4:27

Chapter 5

Strengthening the Gates of Access

Controlling What Comes In And What Goes Out Of Your Life

"Lift up your heads, O you gates! And be lifted up, you everlasting doors! And the King of glory shall come in." — Psalm 24:7 (NKJV)

Gates Are Portals of Permission

Every wall has gates. Gates are not breaches—they are *designed* openings that permit access by *permission*. In biblical times, gates were the place of governance, transaction, and communication. The health of a city was often determined by the strength and condition of its gates.

In your life, gates represent **areas of access**: your mind, mouth, eyes, ears, relationships, and spiritual practices. If you don't control the gates, something else—or someone else—will.

You Are the Gatekeeper of Your Life

As a believer, you are called to *steward* what enters and exits your life.

- **What You Hear (Ear Gate): "Take heed what you hear."** **(Mark 4:24 - NKJV).** Conversations, music, and voices shape your belief system.

- **What You See (Eye Gate)**: **"I will set nothing wicked thing before my eyes." (Psalm 101:3 - NKJV).** Guard your vision—it affects your perception of truth.

- **What You Speak (Mouth Gate)**: **"Death and life are in the power of the tongue." (Proverbs 18:21 - NKJV).** Your words are spiritual weapons.

- **What You Entertain (Heart Gate)**: Whatever you allow into your soul will influence your spirit and behavior.

God has placed the authority of gatekeeping in *your* hands. You decide what enters your home, mind, and spirit.

When the Gates Are Unattended

Unattended gates create dangerous vulnerabilities. If you leave your gate unguarded:

- The enemy sneaks in undetected (**see John 10:10**).
- Unfiltered information pollutes your thinking.
- Bitterness, fear, lust, and lies begin to reside where truth once ruled.
- You lose spiritual sensitivity and discernment.

Ezekiel 44:23 shows the role of the priests: **"And they shall teach My people the difference between the holy and the unholy, and cause them to discern between the unclean and the clean." (NKJV).** This is gatekeeping in action.

Strategic Gatekeeping Requires Discernment

Every gate is not evil, but not every gate is *right* for every season. Sometimes a gate must be temporarily shut to regain strength, clarity, and peace. Other times, a gate must be opened to let in divine relationships, new opportunities, or healing.

Ask yourself:

- What am I allowing in that's weakening me?
- What am I speaking that is empowering the enemy?
- What gates have I opened that God is telling me to close?
- What gates is God trying to open that I'm afraid to step through?

Gatekeeping requires not only guarding, but *discerning*.

Let the King of Glory In

While the enemy seeks access, so does God. The difference is—God waits for permission. He doesn't force His way into your life. That's why Psalm 24:7 says, **"Lift up your heads, O you gates..."** **(NKJV)**—it's a call to **voluntarily open** your spiritual gates to the King of Glory.

When you lift your gates to Him:

- He floods your life with presence and peace.
- He brings order, healing, and revelation.
- He takes His rightful seat at the center of your heart.
- He empowers you to strengthen the gates for future battles.

Securing the Gates for Generations

Your gatekeeping impacts more than just you—it affects your family, legacy, and spiritual community. A strong gatekeeper produces strong children, strong leaders, and strong churches.

Nehemiah 3 records how families were assigned specific gates to repair. It was a **collective responsibility**, and the future of the city depended on each person securing their section.

In the same way, God is calling you to secure your gate, strengthen your section, and protect your border—not just for today, but for the generations to come.

Scriptures for Meditation

- Psalm 24:7–10
- Proverbs 4:23
- Mark 4:24
- Ezekiel 44:23
- Nehemiah 3:1–13
- Revelation 3:20
- Proverbs 18:21
- Psalm 141:3

Chapter 6

Strengthening the Gates of Access

Controlling What Comes In And Out Of Your Life

"Lift up your heads, O you gates... and the King of glory shall come in." — Psalm 24:7 (NKJV)

Every wall that surrounds a territory must have gates. Gates determine access—they either allow entry or enforce restriction. Spiritually, the gates of your life represent the areas where external influence comes in: your mind, eyes, ears, heart, and relationships.

You are the gatekeeper. The enemy cannot invade what you do not permit. But when the gates are left unguarded—through sin, compromise, or spiritual laziness—access is granted to the enemy. That's why **Proverbs 4:23** says, **"Keep your heart with all diligence, for out of it spring the issues of life." (NKJV).**

Gates must be intentionally fortified through prayer, the Word, worship, and consecration. If you don't protect your gates, your peace, purpose, and power are at risk. But when you choose to lift your gates to the Lord—when you open your spirit to Him—He comes in with glory, strength, and authority to take over the territory of your life.

Nehemiah and his people didn't just rebuild the walls—they restored the gates. Your assignment isn't just to defend—it's to discern, rebuild, and grant access only to what honors God.

29

Scriptures for Reflection

- Psalm 24:7–10
- Proverbs 4:23
- Nehemiah 3:1–6
- Matthew 6:22
- Revelation 3:20

Chapter 7

Strengthening the Gates of Access

Controlling What Comes In and Out of Your Life

"Lift up your heads, O you gates; and be lifted up, you everlasting doors! And the King of glory shall come in." — Psalm 24:7 (NKJV)

Gates represent control points—they determine what enters and what exits. In biblical times, city gates were more than entryways. They were places of business, legal rulings, leadership decisions, and spiritual exchange. Whoever controlled the gates had influence over the entire city.

In your spiritual life, the gates represent your mind, emotions, eyes, ears, mouth, and relationships. These access points are either guarded by spiritual discipline or left open to whatever seeks entry—good or evil.

The enemy doesn't need to tear down your wall if he can simply **enter through an unguarded gate**. A distracted mind, a wounded heart, or undisciplined habits can leave a gate wide open. Proverbs 4:23 says, **"Keep your heart with all diligence, for out of it spring the issues of life." (NKJV).**

When we allow fear, sin, compromise, or ungodly influences to enter through these gates, we begin to lose our peace, focus, and spiritual authority. But when we choose to **strengthen our gates**, we begin to take back control of our territory.

31

Strengthening your gates means being intentional about what you watch, listen to, think about, speak, and allow into your atmosphere. It means denying access to the enemy and **welcoming the presence of God**.

When we lift our gates to Him, as Psalm 24 declares, the King of Glory comes in—not just to visit, but to dwell and to defend.

Scriptures for Reflection

- Psalm 24:7–10
- Nehemiah 3:1–6
- Proverbs 4:23
- Revelation 3:20
- Matthew 6:22–23

Chapter 8

Reinforcing Your Walls Through Prayer and Fasting

Spiritual Disciplines That Build Protection, Power, And Perseverance

"Is this not the fast that I have chosen: to loose the bonds of wickedness... And that you break every yoke?" — Isaiah 58:6 (NKJV)

The Spiritual Power of Walls

Walls are not just barriers—they are **boundaries of protection and identity**. Spiritually, your walls are built with truth, faith, obedience, and devotion to God. When your walls are weak or broken, it becomes easier for the enemy to infiltrate your life with discouragement, temptation, or confusion.

But God has given us tools to **reinforce** and **restore** those walls: prayer and fasting. These are not religious rituals—they are weapons of warfare, methods of intimacy, and acts of surrender.

Prayer: Communication That Builds and Guards

Prayer is more than speaking—it's building. It connects you to the Architect of your spiritual walls. It creates sensitivity to the Holy Spirit and exposes cracks before they become breaches.

- **Prayer as Protection**: "Pray that you may not enter into temptation." (Luke 22:40 - NKJV).

- **Prayer as Positioning**: It positions your spirit to respond, not just react.

- **Prayer as Partnership**: When you pray, heaven partners with earth to enforce divine order.

Prayer strengthens the **interior structure** of your wall. The more you pray, the more secure your atmosphere becomes.

Fasting: The Discipline That Restores and Refines

Fasting is the intentional denial of the flesh to empower the spirit. It repairs what has been damaged by compromise or distraction.

- **Fasting Starves the Flesh**: It silences carnal cravings and re-centers your spirit.

- **Fasting Breaks Chains**: According to Isaiah 58, true fasting loosens the bonds of wickedness and breaks every yoke.

- **Fasting Restores Sensitivity**: It sharpens your hearing and heightens your discernment.

Fasting doesn't move God—it moves *you* into alignment with God's will and strength.

When Prayer and Fasting Work Together

Prayer and fasting are powerful on their own—but unstoppable together. In Mark 9:29, Jesus said, **"This kind can come out by nothing but prayer and fasting." (NKJV).** There are levels of spiritual warfare, breakthrough, and clarity that will only be unlocked when both are combined.

Together they:

- Rebuild broken walls of faith and consecration.
- Close open spiritual gates to the enemy.
- Strengthen your authority to fight for your territory.
- Establish inner peace and divine order.

They are spiritual reinforcements that hold your life together when storms rage and enemies surround.

The Watchman's Assignment: Praying at the Wall

Just like Nehemiah posted watchmen while building the wall, God is calling us to pray and fast as **watchmen**. A watchman isn't just guarding for their own sake—they're protecting the entire city.

Your prayer life isn't only about you—it's covering your family, church, community, and even future generations. Watchmen are sensitive, alert, and ready to blow the trumpet at the first sign of danger (**see Ezekiel 33:6**).

When you stand on the wall in prayer and fasting, you're not just surviving—you're *securing*.

Consecration: Keeping the Walls Strong

Walls once built must be **maintained**. Prayer and fasting are not just emergency tools—they are lifestyles of consecration. Regular communion with God preserves the borders of your life and keeps your spiritual gates tightly locked to the enemy.

Consecration isn't legalism—it's loyalty. It's saying, "I value this wall too much to leave it unguarded." It's the decision to **protect your spiritual boundaries daily** through intentional intimacy with God.

Scriptures for Meditation

- Isaiah 58:6–12
- Nehemiah 4:7–9
- Mark 9:29
- Luke 22:40
- Joel 2:12–13
- Ezekiel 33:6
- Psalm 91:1
- Matthew 6:6, 16–18

Chapter 9

Watchmen on the Wall – The Power of Discernment

Appointing Spiritual Guards In Every Area Of Your Life

"I have set watchmen on your walls, O Jerusalem; they shall never hold their peace day or night." — Isaiah 62:6 (NKJV)

The Role of the Watchman in Scripture

In ancient cities, walls were only as effective as the watchmen placed upon them. Watchmen were strategic—positioned to see what others could not. Their job was to sound the alarm at the first sign of danger, ensuring the people were not caught off guard.

Spiritually, **God is still calling for watchmen**—believers who are discerning, alert, and prayerful. A watchman sees what others miss, prays when others sleep, and speaks truth when others are silent. In Ezekiel 33:7, God says, **"So you, son of man: I have made you a watchman for the house of Israel; therefore you shall hear a word from My mouth and warn them for Me."** (NKJV).

Discernment: The Eyes of the Watchman

You cannot be a watchman without discernment. Discernment is the spiritual ability to perceive truth from error, danger from opportunity, and divine timing from human impulse.

- **Discernment Detects the Enemy**: The enemy often appears subtly. Without discernment, deception looks like truth, and delay feels like denial.

- **Discernment Guards the Gates**: It helps you know what to allow into your life—and what to reject.

- **Discernment is Grown in God's Presence**: The more time you spend with God, the clearer your spiritual sight becomes.

Hebrews 5:14 says discernment comes from *constant use*—spiritual maturity sharpens your ability to distinguish good from evil.

Areas That Require Watchmen

Not every area of your life needs a wall, but **every wall needs a watchman**. You must assign spiritual guards to critical areas:

- **Your Family**: Pray over your spouse, children, and home.

- **Your Mind**: Be alert to thought patterns and emotional attacks.

- **Your Ministry**: Guard the purity of your calling and platform.

- **Your Relationships**: Detect unhealthy alignments before they sabotage your peace.

- **Your Church or Community**: Stand in intercession for revival, unity, and divine protection.

A lack of spiritual watchmen can lead to unnecessary warfare, delayed purpose, and spiritual compromise.

The Cost of Silence and Sleep

A watchman who refuses to speak or who sleeps during their assignment opens the door to destruction. Isaiah 56:10 rebukes leaders who are "blind," "mute dogs," and "lazy." These are the types of watchmen who **see but do not speak**, or who **sleep through the warning signs**.

The consequence? What could have been prevented becomes a crisis.

God is looking for faithful watchmen—those who *stand in the gap* and refuse to remain silent even when the warning is unpopular.

Praying from the Wall

Prayer is the primary weapon of the watchman. It's how we alert heaven and resist hell. True watchmen don't just *observe*—they *intervene*.

- **Intercessory Prayer**: You stand in the gap between what is and what God wants to be.

- **Prophetic Prayer**: You declare what God reveals over situations before they manifest.

- **Warfare Prayer**: You bind, resist, and confront spiritual attacks before they take root.

Watchmen understand that **prayer is the first response**, not the last resort.

Becoming a Faithful Watchman

You don't need a title or a pulpit to be a watchman. You simply need a **burden, a heart for truth, and a commitment to intercession**. Becoming a faithful watchman means:

- Keeping your spiritual eyes open.
- Watching not just for danger, but for what God is doing.
- Warning others with love and wisdom.
- Refusing to fall asleep in times of spiritual battle.
- Staying consistent in prayer, even when nothing seems urgent.

Who Will Stand on the Wall?

In every generation, God looks for someone who will say, *"I will stand my post."* Will you be the one who watches over your home, church, calling, and border? The strength of your wall is only as reliable as the faithfulness of the watchman upon it.

Scriptures for Meditation

- Isaiah 62:6–7
- Ezekiel 33:7
- Hebrews 5:14
- 1 Peter 5:8

- Isaiah 56:10
- Matthew 26:41
- Nehemiah 4:9
- 2 Samuel 18:24–27

Chapter 10

Restoring Family Borders

Fighting For The Hedge Around Your Home And Generational Legacy

"Have You not made a hedge around him, around his household, and around all that he has on every side?" — Job 1:10 (NKJV)

The Family: God's First Institution of Order

Before there was a church, temple, or nation, there was **family**. God created the family as the first structure of identity, nurture, and dominion. That's why Satan fights it so viciously. He understands that if he can breach the family border, he can infiltrate every other area of a person's life.

Family borders are not just about physical safety—they are spiritual shields of **identity, purpose, emotional security, and generational alignment**. When these borders are broken, confusion, dysfunction, and cycles of destruction often follow.

The Role of the Family Gatekeeper

Every family needs spiritual gatekeepers—men and women who stand between heaven and earth on behalf of their bloodline.

- **Parents as Protectors**: Fathers and mothers are anointed to discern, guard, and guide.

- **Spouses as Shields**: Husbands and wives must fight together, not just for each other, but for their household.

- **Intercessors as Watchmen**: Even if you are the only believer in your family, God can use you to build a hedge of prayer and declare restoration.

Gatekeepers are those who **say no to generational curses and yes to generational blessings.**

How the Hedge Around the Home Is Broken

Family borders are breached in both subtle and obvious ways:

- **Compromise in Values**: When God's Word is no longer the standard, the foundation weakens.

- **Unforgiveness and Offense**: Bitterness and strife open the door to division.

- **Neglect of Spiritual Leadership**: When no one is praying, teaching, or leading, the enemy fills the void.

- **Generational Sin and Trauma**: Unaddressed wounds and patterns silently weaken the walls of the home.

Just like Jerusalem's walls were burned and torn down (**see Nehemiah 1:3**), many families today are spiritually exposed, unguarded, and vulnerable.

Rebuilding the Hedge with Prayer and Purpose

No matter how damaged your family borders may be, **restoration is possible**. God is a Master Rebuilder.

- **Start with Repentance**: Acknowledge the breach and ask God to restore what's been lost.

- **Establish a Culture of Prayer**: Make your home a dwelling place for God's presence.

- **Teach God's Word**: Deuteronomy 6:7 commands us to teach our children diligently.

- **Renounce Generational Strongholds**: Declare the blood of Jesus over every cycle of addiction, fear, divorce, poverty, or rebellion.

Like Nehemiah, rise up with a tool in one hand and a sword in the other and begin rebuilding.

The Power of a Praying Household

When a family prays together, they build spiritual walls that are not easily shaken. A praying home becomes:

- A fortress of peace.
- A haven of healing.
- A launching pad for purpose.
- A guard post for future generations.

Psalm 127:1a reminds us: **"Unless the Lord builds the house, they labor in vain who build it." (NKJV).** The strength of the home is not in the size of its walls, but in the depth of its foundation.

Defending the Next Generation

Your fight to restore family borders isn't just for today—it's for your children and your children's children. You are standing in the gap to protect **destinies, dreams, and divine callings**.

- **Pray prophetically over your children.**
- **Set spiritual standards in your household.**
- **Break agreements with cultural compromise.**
- **Raise up a legacy of worship, wisdom, and warfare.**

Your children will thank you for the walls you built, even if they didn't understand the battles you fought.

A Family Fortified by Faith

A protected family is a powerful family. God is calling you to take your position at the gates of your home—to build, to guard, and to pray. Whether you're restoring a broken marriage, protecting your children, or breaking generational chains, you are the **watchman, the intercessor, and the builder**.

Don't let the enemy decide what happens in your household. Take authority. Raise the standard. Restore the border.

Scriptures for Meditation

- Job 1:10

- Nehemiah 1:3
- Deuteronomy 6:6–7
- Psalm 127:1
- Isaiah 58:12
- Proverbs 22:6
- Joshua 24:15
- 2 Chronicles 7:14

Chapter 11

Defending Your Territory Against the Enemy

Waging War With Divine Authority to Protect What God Has Entrusted to You

"For the weapons of our warfare are not carnal but mighty in God for pulling down strongholds." — 2 Corinthians 10:4 (NKJV)

You Have a Territory Assigned by God

Every believer has been given a **spiritual territory**—a domain of influence, responsibility, and inheritance. It may include your personal life, family, ministry, business, or calling. God doesn't assign territory without intention. When He places you somewhere, He equips you to **govern, protect, and expand** it.

But with territory comes warfare. The moment you begin to build, advance, or obey, expect resistance.

The Enemy Seeks Unauthorized Access

Satan cannot steal what you do not surrender, but he is always **looking for a weakness**. He prowls, looking for unguarded doors, emotional vulnerability, spiritual laziness, or moments of doubt. His goal is to occupy what belongs to you.

- **He wants your peace.**
- **He wants your family.**
- **He wants your influence and anointing.**
- **He wants to bring division where God intended unity.**

But God has not called you to be a spiritual refugee. He has called you to **defend your ground with boldness and authority**.

Recognizing the Tactics of the Enemy

Before you defend, you must **discern**. The enemy does not always come with red horns—he often disguises his attacks.

- **Distraction**: He pulls your focus from your assignment.

- **Deception**: He twists truth and makes compromise seem acceptable.

- **Discouragement**: He weakens your resolve through exhaustion or delay.

- **Division**: He separates unity to conquer more easily.

- **Despair**: He makes you believe your efforts are in vain.

Your ability to identify these tactics helps you **shut down attacks before they manifest**.

Fight with Spiritual Weapons

God has given you powerful, supernatural weapons designed for victory:

- **The Word of God**: Your sword (**see Hebrews 4:12.**)

- **Prayer and Intercession**: Your communication and authority line.

- **Fasting**: Weakening the flesh and strengthening the spirit.

- **Praise**: A weapon that confuses the enemy (**see 2 Chronicles 20:22**).

- **Faith**: The shield that extinguishes every fiery dart (**see Ephesians 6:16**).
  .

- **The Name and Blood of Jesus**: Your access to divine authority.

These weapons are not symbolic—they are spiritual realities that must be activated daily.

Set Boundaries and Defend Them Boldly

Just as Nehemiah refused to come down from the wall (**see Nehemiah 6:3**), you must learn to **say no to distractions** and **yes to your post**. Some conversations, relationships, and environments must be cut off—not because you're fearful, but because you're focused.

To defend your border means:

- Not tolerating what God told you to cast out.
- Not allowing fear to replace faith.

- Not giving up ground that you've already won.

You are not just a builder—you are a warrior with a responsibility to **enforce heaven's will on earth.**

Defending Doesn't Always Mean Fighting Alone

While spiritual battles are personal, you are not meant to **war in isolation.** God raises up divine allies to strengthen you—pastors, intercessors, friends in the faith. Moses had Aaron and Hur to lift up his arms **(see Exodus 17:12).**

Ask for help. Surround yourself with those who see your assignment and are willing to **fight beside you** in prayer and support.

Victory Belongs to the Defender

You don't need to reclaim your territory—you just need to **defend what already belongs to you.** The land is yours. The anointing is yours. The peace, the purpose, the promises—they are yours.

But they must be defended.

Draw your sword. Guard your gates. Stand your ground. Victory is already written in your favor.

Scriptures for Meditation

- 2 Corinthians 10:4–5
- Ephesians 6:10–18
- Nehemiah 6:3

- 2 Chronicles 20:22
- Exodus 17:8–13
- Joshua 1:3
- 1 Peter 5:8–9
- Isaiah 54:17

Chapter 12

Living Within God's Boundaries for Divine Blessing

The Rewards of Obediently Maintaining God-given Borders in Every Area of Life

"If you are willing and obedient, you shall eat the good of the land." — Isaiah 1:19 (NKJV)

Boundaries Are Not Limitations—They Are Blessings

The world often sees boundaries as restrictions, but in the kingdom of God, **boundaries are blessings in disguise.** They protect the soul, preserve your purpose, and position you to receive divine favor.

God's boundaries are drawn from His love. He doesn't say "no" to restrict your freedom—He says "no" to **preserve your future.** When you live within the lines He has drawn, you experience peace, safety, joy, and clarity.

Psalm 16:6 declares, **"The lines have fallen to me in pleasant places; Yes, I have a good inheritance." (NKJV).**

Obedience Is the Key to Boundary-Based Blessing

Divine blessings are not random—they are **conditional upon obedience.** Throughout scripture, we see God's pattern: where there is obedience to His Word, there is the release of His provision, protection, and presence.

- **Deuteronomy 28:1–2 says, "If you diligently obey... all these blessings shall come upon you..." (NKJV).**

- **Obedience builds trust**—it says, *"I believe God knows better than I do."*

- **Obedience maintains the wall**—it reinforces the spiritual structure of your life.

When you step outside the boundaries of God's instruction, you may find yourself **outside the flow of His provision.**

Boundaries in Relationships: Guarding the Heart and Soul

One of the most powerful areas where boundaries are tested is in relationships. Whether in friendships, marriage, leadership, or mentorship, God's Word sets standards for how we connect.

- Guard against toxic soul ties.
- Set spiritual, emotional, and physical limits in dating and marriage.
- Avoid unequal yokes that pull you out of purpose (**see 2 Corinthians 6:14**).

When God's boundaries are honored, relationships flourish. When they're ignored, even good connections can become dangerous distractions.

Boundaries in Time, Energy, and Focus

You were not created to be accessible to everyone, everywhere, all the time. Jesus Himself practiced boundaries. He pulled away to rest, to pray, and to hear the Father (**see Luke 5:16**).

- **Sabbath is a boundary**—a divine pause for restoration.

- **Purpose-driven focus is a boundary**—saying no to what's good so you can say yes to what's God.

- **Personal health and clarity require boundaries**—without them, burnout is inevitable.

Respecting your time and energy is not selfish—it's strategic.

The Danger of Boundary Violation

Ignoring God's boundaries can lead to:

- **Spiritual depletion**
- **Moral failure**
- **Disconnection from divine protection**
- **Delays in destiny**

Adam and Eve lost Eden by crossing a line God told them not to touch (**see Genesis 2:16–17**). Saul lost his kingdom because he stepped out of his assigned role (**see 1 Samuel 13:13–14**). Anointing cannot cover what **rebellion uncovers**.

Blessing Comes to Those Who Stay in Position

Your greatest blessing is not outside of God's will—it's **right inside His boundary**. Stay where He planted you. Stay faithful. Stay focused. Stay holy.

- The widow's oil flowed **within the vessel boundaries (see 2 Kings 4:5–6)**.

- The provision for Ruth came because she stayed **in Boaz's field (see Ruth 2:8–9)**.

- Jesus taught that the sheep who remained in the fold were the ones the shepherd guarded **(see John 10:1–4)**.

God blesses those who choose to **live within the lines** of His love, His law, and His leading.

Border Blessings Are Real

Every chapter of this book has been building toward this: when you protect and strengthen your border, **you position yourself for sustained, supernatural blessing**. The walls you build, the gates you guard, the discernment you develop, and the boundaries you respect all work together to ensure you remain under divine covering.

Live in obedience. Stay within the territory God has given you. And watch how He releases favor, fruitfulness, and fulfillment that no enemy can stop.

Scriptures for Meditation

- Isaiah 1:19
- Psalm 16:6
- Deuteronomy 28:1–14
- John 10:1–4
- 2 Kings 4:5–6
- Genesis 2:16–17
- Ruth 2:8–9
- Proverbs 3:5–6

Conclusion

The Border Is Sacred — Guard It with Your Life

Throughout this book, we've journeyed through the landscape of natural and spiritual borders—walls that protect, gates that regulate, and territories that God has entrusted into our care. From Nehemiah's burden to rebuild the wall, to Job's hedge of divine protection, to Jesus' call to watch and pray, one truth has remained central: **your border matters.**

Your spiritual borders are more than symbolic—they are life-defining. They shape your decisions, guard your relationships, defend your legacy, and protect the glory of God that rests upon your life. When you neglect the border, you risk exposure. But when you honor and strengthen it, you make room for blessing, authority, and victory.

We've learned that:

- **Broken walls can be rebuilt.**
- **Gates must be guarded with discernment.**
- **Families need spiritual hedges and watchmen.**
- **Obedience keeps you within the safety of divine boundaries.**
- **You have the power and responsibility to defend your God-given territory.**

This is not just a teaching—it's a call to action.

The days we are living in are dark, and the spiritual climate is intense. Compromise is common, and apathy is widespread. But God is raising up **builders, watchmen, and warriors** who will no longer be passive about the sacred trust they've been given. He's calling you to the wall. He's assigning you to the gate. He's positioning you to **reclaim, reinforce, and revive** every part of your life that has been under siege.

Let this not be the end, but the beginning of your border revival.

Stand firm. Fortify your foundation. And never forget—**what you guard today will determine what you inherit tomorrow.**

The border is sacred. Guard it with your life.

God has trusted you with it. Now rise and protect it.

Scripture Reference Index

Building and Rebuilding Walls

- Nehemiah 1:3–4
- Nehemiah 2:17–20
- Nehemiah 3:1–6
- Nehemiah 4:6–9
- Nehemiah 6:3
- Isaiah 58:12

Guarding Gates and Spiritual Access

- Psalm 24:7–10
- Proverbs 4:23
- Matthew 6:22–23
- Revelation 3:20
- Ezekiel 44:23
- Isaiah 62:6–7

Spiritual Warfare and Defending Territory

- 2 Corinthians 10:4–5
- Ephesians 6:10–18
- 1 Peter 5:8–9
- Joshua 1:3
- Isaiah 54:17
- Exodus 17:8–13
- Luke 22:40
- Mark 9:29

The Role of the Watchman

- Isaiah 62:6–7
- Ezekiel 33:7
- Isaiah 56:10
- 2 Samuel 18:24–27
- Matthew 26:41
- Hebrews 5:14

Family and Generational Protection

- Job 1:10
- Deuteronomy 6:6–7
- Joshua 24:15
- Proverbs 22:6
- Psalm 127:1
- 2 Chronicles 7:14
- Nehemiah 1:3

Prayer, Fasting, and Consecration

- Isaiah 58:6–12
- Joel 2:12–13
- Matthew 6:6, 16–18
- Psalm 91:1
- Hebrews 4:12
- 2 Chronicles 20:22

Obedience and Boundaries

- Isaiah 1:19
- Psalm 16:6
- Deuteronomy 28:1–14

- Genesis 2:16–17
- Ruth 2:8–9
- John 10:1–4
- Proverbs 3:5–6
- 2 Kings 4:5–6
- 1 Samuel 13:13–14
- 2 Corinthians 6:14

www.ingramcontent.com/pod-product-compliance
Lightning Source LLC
LaVergne TN
LVHW021547080426
835509LV00019B/2878

DEDICATION

This book is dedicated to everyone who has been in my life both past and present. For each one of you have shaped a part of me in some way! I thank you all for everything that you've taught to me....

Table of Contents